Changes

Prayers and Services Honoring
Rites of Passage

CHURCH PUBLISHING
an imprint of
Church Publishing Incorporated, New York

Church Publishing Incorporated
445 Fifth Avenue
New York, NY 10016
www.churchpubishing.org

5 4 3 2 1

CONTENTS

PUBLISHER'S NOTE

These Rites of Passage are the work of the Standing Commission on Liturgy and Music of the Episcopal Church. They are a unique combination of prayers and services suitable for use in corporate worship and in the more intimate environment of the family. It is the Publisher's hope that these Rites—addressing a breadth of pastoral situations and needs—will enrich the lives of many congregations, families, and individuals within the Episcopal Church and beyond.

FOREWORD

by The Rt. Rev. Mark MacDonald
Bishop of Alaska

In its primal form, as described by the Evangelists, the gospel was a proclamation unveiling the regal and redeeming presence of God in the everyday life of its hearers. In that gospel encounter, Jesus became—in his life, death, resurrection, and second coming—the matrix for new life and a new world. This would lead, through a change of mind and heart, to a transformation so profound that it would provide a gateway to a new universe. Please note, it is such an expansive vision that informs and animates these Rites of Passage.

The immediate excitement these Rites will generate may obscure the larger significance of this work. There will be immediate and obvious interest in their potential for pastoral care and evangelism. For most of us, the scope and quality of this work will be quickly grasped and applied, firstly in a renewed pastoral and evangelistic imagination, and secondly, in their use in real life situations. But this is only a part of the achievement of the team that produced this work.

I once heard the great priest and scholar Boone Porter describe the vision of the primary architects of the Episcopal Church's 1979 Book of Common Prayer. He said they had placed a number of "land mines" in what we might call the implicit ecclesiology and missiology of the Book. Only a few of these land mines have appeared, since most of us use the current Prayer Book as if it were a supplement to the 1928 Prayer Book. In the same way, many of us used our personal computers as fancy typewriters, without discovering that they are completely new instruments. With joy, we can say that in these Rites of Passage a visionary group of folks have begun to live into the promise and power of a number of the currents of renewal that have been beckoning the church forward over the past fifty years.

The remarkable breadth of these Rites, the increased missiological capacity they create, are the product of many cultural currents running through the life of our church. Like the New Zealand/Aotearoa Prayer Book, they exemplify interculturation (as opposed to inculturation, which refers to the process of the Word of God becoming living, real, and liberating in a single culture). Since the events described in Acts 15, this interculturation has been the lifeblood of the renewal of the church. As the Word becomes flesh in a particular culture, a process of sharing with other cultures—an exchange of perspective, enrichment, and, sometimes, prophetic critique—allows the various ways of life that make up the church universal to transform us into what God intends us to be. In the various facets of gospel life and light, refracted in the living experience of peoples renewed in Christ, we begin to see the first rays of a dawning for the new humanity intended for the church. This is accomplished, when authentic, without losing either individual cultural integrity or our universal communion, both qualities being the essence of the catholicity promised us in Christ.

At a practical level, we are entering a theological perspective that may be new and challenging for many of us. Since the Enlightenment, the churches of the West have tended to limit God's activity and presence within the explicit realm of church belief, teaching, and practice. This focus of institutional presentation and experience fundamentally shaped Western assumptions about the world and cultural competence within it. With the publication of these Rites we enter new cultural perspectives, as well as encountering a broader understanding of God's presence in Creation and in human life. For many of the cultures that now make up our common life in the church, the presence of God also rests in other locations of power and importance: family, home, school, work, and the environment. An amazingly diverse array of theological voices beckons the churches of the West to a broader view of God's presence. These have included Eastern Orthodox theologians; theologians of the margins from many cultures and countries around the world—especially from the aboriginal peoples and Asia; feminist theologians; and, closer to home, voices like William Stringfellow, to name only a few.

We can expect that, at some level, the presentation of these Rites will raise controversy. Some of this will be related, quite simply, to their newness. Some of it will be a part of the useful and necessary process of critical reception that accompanies any new liturgical venture. We must, however, expect some controversy from the prophetic challenge the Rites raise for our common life and missiology. On this level, we will receive a call to more forward.

Orlando Costas (in his 1982 *Christ Outside the Gate: Mission Beyond Christendom*) prophetically noted that the only renewal possible for the North American church would come through the re-evangelization of the churches by the poor, by ethnic minorities, and by immigrants. The ease, power, and idolatry of "Christendom" would mean that any growth apart from such a re-evangelization would be mere "ecclesiastical obesity." Though we may not have entered into that new world in these Rites of Passage, you can see it from here.

⊞

INTRODUCTORY
MATERIALS

⊞

THEOLOGY AND RATIONALE

The Holy Spirit is forever working to renew the whole creation, which "waits with eager longing for the revealing of the children of God" *(Romans 8:19)*. As children of God, we are constantly being called to new life, to be reborn in the image of the one who loves us with eternal love. Always, the Spirit breathes, whispers, and calls, leading us as Christ's body in a dance of transforming grace. Change, then, is inevitable in the lives of God's people. Divine love relentlessly invites us to transformation in the image of Christ. Often, though, we resist the changes our Father asks of us—sometimes, we fall back on the safety of the familiar. Nor are all changes godly. Our gracious Creator allows us freedom of choice—while human sin tempts us to choose badly. Nonetheless, even amid brokenness, tragedy, and the consequences of our bad choices, unexpected grace may witness to the presence and power of the Holy One. Through faith and trust in Christ, we can embrace both the joy and the pain of change, and testify to God's redeeming power.

These rites reflect confidence in God's presence among us throughout the changes and chances of this life. Through prayer and ritual, the Holy Spirit can stretch our hearts in love, leading individuals and the worshiping community into ever greater faith and trust.

Transitions in the Gospel Stories

In the lives of Jesus and his followers, we note major life transitions that made prophets out of carpenters, disciples out of fishermen, evangelists out of broken women. In most cases, these events were witnessed by and celebrated in the company of seekers, revelers, clerics, and skeptics, many of whom were then drawn into an ever-widening community of companionship. Examples to ponder include:

- Mary's presentation of Jesus in the Temple forty days after his birth, with the prophetic and pastoral support of Simeon and Anna—a time of transition for them, as well as for the new family.

- Jesus' teaching in the Temple, when he and his parents became separated and they could not find him. This passage from childhood dependency to a new independence was witnessed and supported by a community on pilgrimage to and from Jerusalem.

- Jesus' baptism into ministry at the River Jordan.

- Simon's recognition and naming of Jesus as the Christ, and his own subsequent re-naming: "You are Peter, now; you are Rock."

- Zacchaeus' change of heart and vocation in his turning from sin, sealed by sitting down with Jesus to break bread.

- The healing of the man born blind, whose redeemed status was sorely tested by the religious authorities.

- Jesus' calling the Samaritan woman to the ministry of evangelism.

- The restoration of the hemorrhaging woman to her worshiping community by Jesus' very public display of healing, in which he redeemed her outcast status and renamed her "Daughter."

- Mary's encounter with Jesus at the empty tomb. In calling her by name, he commissions her to a new mission to go and tell others, "I have seen the Lord."

God Loves Our Humanity

Through the Incarnation in Jesus Christ, God unequivocally embraces the ordinariness of human life: the divine Word came to live inside our common humanity. The Holy Spirit dwells within us every moment of our lives—even when we feel most abandoned by God. This indwelling is our assurance that the holy and undivided Trinity delights in us and cherishes creation. In Eucharistic worship, we turn to God as manifest in glory, to Christ's presence among us in bread and wine, and to the Holy Spirit alive within each of us and present in the fellowship of the gathered community. Here, the Holy One comforts and confronts us through rich tapestries of symbol and sacrament. In liturgies acknowledging and celebrating life's transitions, we affirm that:

- We trust the divine Love to embrace us through all the joys and pains of transition.

- We are so interconnected by the Holy Spirit that a transition in one member's life affects the whole Christian community.

- God is continuously healing and transforming the world. When we join with our Creator in the process of our own transformations, we participate in the coming of Christ's kingdom. So if anyone is in Christ, there is a new creation; everything old has passed away; see, everything has become new! (2 Corinthians 5:17)

Structure and Features

The following rites offer opportunities both to ask for God's blessing and to offer that blessing to the Christian community collectively and on each of its members during moments of significant change in our lives.

Elements of the Rites

Through ritual acts, people of all cultures and religious traditions mark life's course, giving it shared significance and sanctifying it. Rites of passage not only recognize changes that have already happened; they can also effect changes.

Passages from one stage to the next involve three elements:

Rites of separation name what is being left behind, preparing us for new birth.

Rites of transition celebrate the past while anticipating the future. They help us pause to begin the (sometimes lengthy) process of accepting and embracing change.

Rites of reintegration name, sanctify and celebrate one's new status in the community.

While all rites of passage appear to involve this structure, the means and relative emphasis by which the ritual passage is shaped can vary widely.

Each of the following rites seeks to include these key elements or themes:

* Naming the transition: how it affects the person, his/her primary relationships, and the whole community.
* Declaring what went before: loss, growth, gift—then acknowledging grief, letting go, giving thanks.
* Petitioning God for what is needed and sought in the transition: healing, courage, imagination.
* Proclaiming hope for the future, with willingness to discern new ministries.

Structures of the Rites

Please note that these are templates for rites of passage. Lay and ordained leaders should adapt these rites to their particular cultural contexts.

In all of the following rites, we have sought to feature
* clarity of symbol
* simplicity of language
* the invitation to all to continue in the life and work of the worshiping community

Each rite is structured in the familiar pattern of most Prayer Book liturgies with these building blocks:

- Entrance Rite
- The Greeting, the "Dearly Beloved," which reminds us why we are gathered
- The Collect(s)
- The Ministry of the Word: Scripture, Readings, Homilies
- The Presentation and/or Examination
- The Action: Blessing, Naming, Commissioning
- The Prayers or a Litany
- The Option of Holy Communion

The Rites as Related to Stages in Human Development

These rites seek to include the particular needs and focus of the age group for which they are written, using this model of four stages of life, and the special quality or focus of each stage:

Youth: birth to 22: Dependence
Rising Adulthood: ages 22–44: Activity
Midlife: ages 45–66: Leadership
Elders: age 66 and upward: Stewardship

The rites and prayers that follow consider these special life tasks:

- In the Transitions of Childhood, there is growth from dependence to independence. Confidence and courage are sought for the maturing person, and the grace to let go is sought for the adults on whom the young person necessarily relies.

- In the Transitions of Rising Adulthood, the new adult needs to channel activity into God's loving will for all creation by choosing activities that align with his or her own God-given gifts and calling.

- In the Transitions of Midlife, the adult searches for new gifts of leadership which need to be identified, strengthened, and called forth by the community. We are reminded that these gifts are meant to enhance the life of the entire Christian community and the world.

- In Transitions of Later Life, circumstances call for the elder to give back some of what has earlier been received as part of preparing to leave the world a better place for those who will follow.

⊞

Planning for
a Rite of Passage

⊞

Planning for a Rite of Passage

Along with complete rites, prayers and guidelines are provided to help create a rite especially suited to the transitioning person, his or her community, and the cultural context in which the person lives.

Who?

- For what person or group is this rite being prepared?
- Who needs to be included and invited, and how?

What?

- What is the purpose of this rite?
- What needs to happen in it and through it? Using the plainest, most everyday language will help the rite communicate simply, clearly, and effectively.

How?

- How and where will the people gather?
- What should members of the community bring to the celebration?
- Will there be a meal following?
- After this rite, how will life be different for the person in transition and for the community?

The Gathering

- Will there be a procession, whom will it include, and what music (dancing, drumming) will be appropriate?

The Greeting

- Who is most appropriate to explain why we are gathered?
- Will the content of the greeting be selected from the rites below, written for the occasion, or offered informally by a leader of the community?

The Collect

- What Collects or prayers will introduce the Ministry of the Word? Will they be selected from those below or written for the occasion?

The Ministry of the Word

- Will this include Scripture readings, extra-biblical readings, stories, memory sharing, or tributes? Who will offer them?
- Will there be a homily? Who should speak?
- If a Eucharist is part of the celebration, what Gospel reading will be chosen?

The Presentation and Examination
- Will there be a presentation of the person in transition?
- How to tell what led to and preceded this transition, and what is being sought through it (e.g., healing, commissioning, rededication, thanksgiving)?
- Should the person in transition declare in her own voice her intentions, hopes, and new commitments?

The Action
- How will the person be blessed, named, commissioned?
- Who will do the blessing / commissioning?
- Will a formula from this set of rites be used, or will something be written for the occasion, and, if so, by whom?

The order of the Action and the Prayers may be reversed.

The Prayers
- Will one of the forms for the Prayers of the People included in these rites be used?
- Or will a form be chosen from the Book of Common Prayer?
- Or will prayers be written for the occasion? If so, by whom?

The Peace and, When Desired, the Celebration of Holy Eucharist
A Proper Preface

In most of the Rites of Transition, where a Eucharist is celebrated, this Proper Preface will be appropriate.

From day to day, from age to age, throughout our lives in this world and the next, you show yourself to be eternal Love, giver and sustainer of all goodness and joy; and so, with all the saints of every generation who are ancient in faith and young in hope, we join to sing your praise:

The liturgy continues with the Sanctus, "Holy, holy, holy."

⊞

PRAYERS FOR THE TRANSITIONS OF CHILDHOOD

⊞

PRAYERS FOR THE
TRANSITIONS OF CHILDHOOD

These prayers may be used alone or incorporated into a larger rite of passage.

1. Moving from a Crib to a Bed
2. Becoming a Big Brother or Sister
3. Beginning the School Year
4. Ending the School Year
5. Becoming a Reader
6. Learning to Ride a Bike
7. Going Away to Camp
8. When a Friend Moves Away

1. Moving from a Crib to a Bed

The new bed may be made up with the child's help. Members of the household, including the child, may move in procession from the crib to the bed with pillows, blankets, stuffed animals or other objects regularly part of the nighttime ritual.

Good and loving God, your watchful care never slumbers, and you give gifts to your children even as they sleep. Thank you for bringing us all to this day into which *N.* has grown in your protection. Give *her* blessed rest wherever *she* lays *her* head. Keep *her* well and fill *her* dreams with hope. Awaken *her* every morning to the sureness of your love with joy and courage for the day at hand; through Jesus, our Savior and Friend. *Amen.*

2. Becoming a Big Brother or Sister

You call us your children, O God, and through grace and adoption you make us your own. Through the *birth* of a baby to *his* mother *and father, N.* has become a big *brother.* Help *him* to be patient and gentle with *himself* and the baby as *he* learns to share *his* home, *his* parent(s), and *his* toys. Keep this new relationship in your watchful care, so that these children may become lifelong companions in friendship and faith; through Jesus, our Brother and Lord, we pray. *Amen.*

3. Beginning the School Year

Dear God, today is *N.'s* first day of *school* [*First Grade*], a happy, exciting, scary day. We pray that *N.'s* teachers will be generous, wise, and gracious. We pray for *N.'s* classmates, so that true friendships may be found for all. Especially we pray for *N.* Keep *her* safe and well. Open *her* heart and mind to a world of learning, and may this be the first of thousands of days in which *she* knows the depth of your love and the constancy of your care. We pray in Jesus' name. *Amen.*

or this

Child of my heart, may the blessing of the Holy Trinity go with you today.
May God's strength keep you secure.
May Christ our true Wisdom guide your learning.
May the Holy Spirit make you glad and good.
May the enfolding of the Trinity hold you and bring you, at day's end, safely home.
Amen.

4. Ending the School Year

Dear God, we have finished a year of school, and we are thankful. We have been challenged and tested; we have studied and played; we have loved and we have grown. We are ready for a long and joy-filled rest. Bless this school year now ending. Bless our teachers and friends. May our bodies stay well, our hearts and minds open; and may all of our learning help us to serve this world you love so dearly. We pray in Jesus' name. *Amen.*

5. Becoming a Reader

Dear God, our *brother, N.,* has learned to read and now enters the vast world of books. Let his imagination and joy increase and *his* perception of truth grow strong as *he* delights in words, traveling through stories. Remind *him* to read your word in the Bible, and to write its instruction into *his* heart. May *he* learn to read, as well, the sorrows and needs of others, and all the signs of your loving presence in this world you created. We pray in Jesus' name. *Amen.*

6. Learning to Ride a Bike

You move through our lives, O God, like the wind, pushing and pulling us into the adventures of growing up. Our young *sister, N.,* has learned to ride a bicycle, conquering fear, enlarging *her* world, and tasting new freedom and speed. May the learning of this skill teach *her* to risk and to trust, to hold on and to let go, as life demands from day to day, and may *she* be kept safe always. We pray in Jesus' name. *Amen.*

7. Going Away to Camp

In the beauty of your world, O God, you show us how great your love is. Be with *N.* as *he* goes away to camp. Open *his* eyes to the wonder of creation and, in it, let *him* draw nearer to you. Let *his* play be joyful. Let *him* encounter wonder and surprise as he learns. Let *his* rest be peaceful. Keep *N.* well and safe, in the knowledge that *he* is deeply loved by you and by us, who hold *him* dear in our hearts for ever. We pray in Jesus' name. *Amen.*

8. When a Friend Moves Away

There is no place in all the world, O God, where you do not hold us in love. *N.'s* friend is moving away. But as your love can stretch from house to house, from nation to nation, and from heart to heart, so it can keep our friendships strong wherever we may be. Help *N.* and *her* friend, *N.,* as they say goodbye. Comfort their sadness. May the joy they have known with each other last, and ever be found in new friends. We pray in Jesus' name. *Amen.*

⊞

Prayers and Rites
for the Transitions of
Youth and Young Adulthood

⊞

THE PRAYERS

1. Reaching Puberty

Creator of Life, you have formed us in your image, male and female, and we are wonderfully made for the joy of human love. We thank you for this *girl, N.,* whom you have brought to maturity. In the freedom of childhood *she* has come to this time, and *she* needs your grace and guidance for the responsibilities of adulthood. You have designed *her* days for love and for work, for sharing and for growing, for searching and for finding. Keep *her* safe throughout *her* life, and give *her* the courage to follow *her* heart, and walk in your ways; through Jesus, our true Companion in our journey to you. *Amen.*

2. Earning a Driver's License or Permit

Gracious God, our *brother, N.,* has come to an occasion of great privilege and responsibility. In the new freedoms which driving affords *him,* help *N.* to remember all of us who love *him* and are trusting *him* to drive safely, wisely, and kindly. In all the journeys of *his* life, go with *him* and bear *him* up with your sheltering love. And may this adventure be only one of thousands in which your gifts of freedom and care go hand-in-hand to bless *him*; through Jesus Christ our Savior. *Amen.*

3. Dating Relationships

Our greatest joy in life, O God, is to love. We thank you for showing us through Jesus that loving a child, a friend, a dream, or a companion makes us more fully human, created in your image. As *N.* stands ready to begin dating, help *her* to remember that *she* will be learning that love is sacred. May *she* bring to each new date hope for a true friendship. May *she* listen, and speak, and act with the greatest respect for *herself* and her companion. May *she* strive for a relationship that is truthful, patient, courageous, and kind. Above all, may love teach *her* to love you more and more as, through the Spirit's care, *she* grows in the image of your holy child, Jesus Christ our Redeemer. *Amen.*

4. Graduating from High School

In every beginning is an ending, O Lord, and in every end something new begins. Our *brother, N.,* has graduated from high school, and is ready now for new learning and experiences. Grant that childhood's innocence and hope may remain alive in *him*, bringing joy as *he* matures. Grant that *he* may hear your still small voice in *his* heart saying, "This is the way; walk in it." Help *him* preserve old friendships while creating new ones. Grant that we who love *him* may help *him* to find *his* own voice, *his* own words and *his* own work in Christ's true way, who knows the person *he* was created to be; we pray this in Jesus' name. *Amen.*

5. Going to College

Gracious God, your Holy Spirit instructs our hearts in the ways of life. In going to college, your child *N.,* has set aside a time of learning and preparation for *her* life's work. Through all the years ahead, make *her* hungry for wisdom tempered with love. Help *her* discern the truth in all that *she* learns, in the people *she* meets, and in the choices *she* must face each day. Keep *her* mind alert for the rigors of study and exams. Keep *her* body safe and well. Giver *her* a heart bold to question, yet alive to your wonders. And assure *her* always of your love and ours; through Christ, your Wisdom made flesh. *Amen.*

6. Joining the Workforce

Holy God, you call us to work as friends of Jesus, who was sent among us to serve and reconcile. As *N.* enters the workforce, bless *him* with wisdom and skill. May the work of *his* hands bring *him* satisfaction. May *he* be faithful, honest, and fair with all who labor beside *him*, and may they be so with *him*. In all that *he* does, may *he* glorify Christ, whose saving work on the cross brings us to rest in your love, and through whom we pray. *Amen.*

7. Going on a Pilgrimage

Holy One, you led your people, night and day, by fire and cloud, so lead *N.* (*N.,* *N.,*) by the light of your love. Go before *him* to prepare a safe path. Stay beside *him* to instill purpose and joy in *his* mission. Follow after *him* to leave peace in the wake of wherever *he* has stayed. Give your angels charge over *his* journey. At *his* returning, may all *he* has seen be engraved on *his* heart, and *his* sense of home enlarged for ever; through Jesus Christ, our Savior and Guide. *Amen.*

8. Moving from the Family Home

Your Spirit, O God, keeps us moving ever forward in faith as you call us to new places and new beginnings. Your servant *N.* is leaving the home of *her* childhood to a home of *her* own. We give thanks for *her* newfound independence and the courage to care for *herself.* May the place *she* is leaving withstand *her* loss. May the home *she* is creating become a place of shelter and peace. And may we all come to know our true and eternal home in your heart; through Christ our Lord. *Amen.*

A RITE OF PASSAGE FOR
YOUNG PEOPLE AND THEIR PARENTS

The journey through adolescence often challenges both young people and their parents. The parish community can affirm and uphold them through this journey.

This rite is appropriate for an individual or for a group of young people. It may be used to mark graduation from elementary school, entrance into middle school, or turning 13.

Entrance Rite

In the opening procession, each young person is joined by family. They are seated together at the front of the assembly. Suggestions for hymns and spiritual songs are listed on pp. 29-30.

Opening Acclamation

Presider	Blessed be God who has brought us to this day.
People	Blessed be the God of all our days.
Presider	Thanks be to Jesus who restores us to wholeness.
People	Thanks be to Jesus in whose death is our life.
Presider	Praise to the Spirit who calls us to service.
People	Praise to the Spirit who leads us in love.

Collect

Presider	The Lord be with you.
People	And also with you.
Presider	Let us pray.

Holy God, in you we live and move and have our being: Grant to all your people the courage to live gracefully through the changes and chances of life, giving thanks for your guiding Spirit and your never-failing love; through Jesus Christ our Lord, who with you and the Holy Spirit, lives and reigns for ever and ever. *Amen.*

The Ministry of the Word

Suggested readings are listed on p. 28.

A homily may follow the readings.

The Presentation and Examination

Dear People of God: Throughout life's journey we encounter moments of change that call us to grow. In the relationship between parent and child there are many such moments of challenge and grace. Though each of these has unique burdens and joys, adolescence especially requires greater patience, forgiveness, courage, and hope. Parent and child must learn to risk and to let go. These children and their parents come to this faithful community to offer thanks for all that has been, and to seek God's blessing for all their futures. We join them in acknowledging and celebrating the transition as they stand on the threshold.

Who is ready to begin this new phase of life?

Parents and children present each other, one family group at a time. Godparents and other significant adults may also stand with the parents and children.

Young Person These are my parents, N. and N., who have raised me and love me.

or

This is my mother/father, N., who has raised me and loves me.

Parents This is our son/daughter N., whom we love with all our heart.

or

Parent This is my son/daughter N., whom I love with all my heart.

Young person and parent(s) together

We stand before God and before our faithful community to acknowledge that we are in the midst of a change that calls us to fresh ways of understanding one another. Help us be thankful for all that has been and for all that is to come. We trust God's constant love and pray a blessing for this time of transition.

The Presider addresses the young people and adults, saying

N., N., [and N.], you are made in the image of God who has held you in love every day of your life, and always will. Remember your divine Maker who formed you in joy and remolds you for the changes that lie before you. The Creator who knows you delights in the work that prepares you for your roles in Christ's healing of the world.

The Presider addresses the young people, saying

N., [N., and N.], will you continue to honor your parents, respecting their life experience, and remembering their love for you?

Young People I will, with God's help

Presider Will you strive to make decisions that honor your body, your spirit, and your relationships?

Young People I will, with God's help

The Presider addresses the parents, saying

N., [N., and N.], in the sacred responsibility of giving and sustaining life, you reflect the image of God. These children are God's gifts to you, as truly as you are God's gifts to them. Remember that God has never forsaken you, and will always be near, in this and in every good work to which you are called, for which you respond in faith. Know that you are ministers of God's love to these young people.

Will you respect the dignity of your *sons and daughters,* listening to all that *they* tell you, even allowing *them* to make their own mistakes when you may responsibly do so?

Parents	I will, with God's help.
Presider	Will you set limits and spacious boundaries for these young people, intended to keep *them* safe and well?
Parents	I will, with God's help.

Presider, to parents and young people
> Will all of you be patient with yourselves and each other, practicing forgiveness and forbearance, and holding fast to love's courage, joy, and hope?

Young People and Parents
> We will, with God's help.

Presider Will you remember to include the outcast, love the lonely, and practice mercy?

Young People and Parents
> We will, with God's help.

Presider Will you be faithful in attending church, studying the Scriptures, and saying your prayers?

Young People and Parents
> We will, with God's help.

Presider, to the People
> Will you as their Christian community support these young people and their parents during their time of change and growth?

Congregation We will. We welcome your presence among us, honoring the gifts of insight and freshness you bring us. We will sing and pray with you. We will challenge you to be generous and compassionate as you serve Christ in your home, at church, and in the world. Will you do the same for us?

Young People and Parents
> We will, with God's help.

The use of these Prayers for the Candidates at Baptism in The Book of Common Prayer are suggested, using this introduction and concluding collect in place of those in the Prayer Book.

Let us now pray for *these young persons* who seek God's blessing and ours as *they* journey into adulthood.

A Person appointed leads the following petitions

Leader	Deliver *them*, O Lord, from the way of sin and death.
People	Lord, hear our prayer.
Leader	Open *their hearts* to your grace and truth.
People	Lord, hear our prayer.
Leader	Fill *them* with your holy and life-giving Spirit.
People	Lord, hear our prayer.
Leader	Keep *them* in the faith and communion of your holy Church.
People	Lord, hear our prayer.
Leader	Teach *them* to love others in the power of the Spirit.
People	Lord, hear our prayer.
Leader	Send *them* into the world in witness to your love.
People	Lord, hear our prayer.
Leader	Bring *them* to the fullness of your peace and glory.
People	Lord, hear our prayer.

At the conclusion of the prayers

Grant, O Lord, that *this young person*, who was baptized into the death of Jesus Christ your Son, may continue *her* earthly pilgrimage in the power of his resurrection, and may wait in hope for his coming again in glory, who lives and reigns now and for ever. *Amen.*

In place of these prayers, others may be written for the occasion.

The Blessing
The people may gather round and lay hands on the young people and their parents, as the Presider offers this blessing.

All-holy God, source of every blessing: We thank you for the mystery of growing up, the transformation of body, mind, and spirit that brings children to adulthood. We marvel in this and all your works. Give *these parents and young people* grace and courage, patience and good humor, respect and compassion, and unfailing hope, as they travel together through life, sisters and brothers united in Christ and his household, the Church. We pray in Jesus' name. *Amen.*

The service continues with the Peace and, if desired, the celebration of the Eucharist.
This Preface may be used at the Eucharist.

From day to day, from age to age, throughout our lives in this world and the next, you show yourself to be eternal Love, giver and sustainer of all goodness and joy; and so, with all the saints of every generation who are ancient in faith and young in hope, we join to sing your praise:

Suggested Readings

1 Samuel 3:1–10	(The calling of Samuel)
Isaiah 61:1–3	(The Spirit of the Lord is upon me)
Proverbs 2:1–5	(If you make your ear attentive to wisdom)
Proverbs 3:13–18	(Happy are those who find wisdom)
Proverbs 6:20–22	(Keep your father's commandment and your mother's teaching)
Joel 2:28c–29	(I will pour out my spirit on all flesh)

Psalm 22:9–10	(It was you who took me from my mother's womb)
Psalm 23	(The Lord is my shepherd)
Psalm 70:5–6, 17–18	(You are my trust from my youth)
Psalm 119:9–16	(How can young people keep their way pure?)
Psalm 139:1–18	(You knit me together in my mother's womb)

Romans 8:14–17	(All who are led by the Spirit of God are children of God)
1 Corinthians 13	(When I was a child)
Ephesians 4:11–16	(Until we all attain to the measure of the stature of the fullness of Christ)
Philippians 4:4–9	(Whatever is true, honorable. . . think on these things. . . and the God of peace will be with you)
1 Timothy 4:11–16	(Let no one despise your youth)

Luke 2:41–52	(Jesus, as a boy, in the Temple)

Suggested Hymns and Spiritual Songs

More suggestions are found on pp. 79-82.

From *The Hymnal 1982*

611	Christ, the worker
490	I want to walk as a child of the light
549, 550	Jesus calls us
602	Jesu, Jesu
587	Our Father, by whose Name
599	Lift every voice and sing
482	Lord of all hopefulness
554	'Tis the gift to be simple

From *Lift Every Voice and Sing II*

16	You are near
52	God has smiled on me
59	My heavenly father watches over me
65	Bless the Lord
70	I want Jesus to walk with me
76	Jesus in the morning
91	Give me Jesus
100	Somebody's Knockin'
106	Precious Lord
111	Come thou fount of every blessing
131	I know the Lord's laid his hands on me
136	I have decided to follow Jesus
160	This little light of mine
177	Standin' in the need of prayer
189	Great is thy faithfulness
194	Lead me, guide me
213	Children of the heavenly Father
214	God is so good
216	In my life Lord, be glorified
218	Jesus loves me
219	This is the day that the Lord has made
220	Jacob's ladder
221	This little light of mine
231	Choral benediction
232	Thank you Lord
189	Great is thy faithfulness

128	Hush, hush, somebody's callin' my name
191	His eye is on the sparrow
747	God, the sculptor of the mountains
819	Guide my feet, Lord

From *Wonder, Love, and Praise*

812	I, the Lord of sea and sky
742	Loving Spirit
770	O God of gentle strength
757	Will you come and follow me

From other sources

I was there to hear your borning cry (Fortress Press)
Sanctuary (Full Armor Music and Whole Armor Music)
Bless now, O God, the journey (*Voices Found*)
Make me a channel of your peace (Oregon Catholic Press)
We Are Called, Come, Live in the Light (GIA)
You are Mine (GIA)
Bind us Together (Kingsway's Thank You Music)
We are not our own (New Century Hymnal)

A RITE OF PASSAGE
FOR A SIGNIFICANT BIRTHDAY

This rite is intended for young men and women celebrating a significant birthday in their journey to adulthood. The age will vary, depending on the community. Many cultures have long celebrated Quinceañera (a girl's fifteenth birthday), Fiesta Clavel (a boy's fifteenth birthday), Sweet Sixteen, Debut, or Coming of Age.

This rite affirms God's presence, continued blessing, guidance for the future. Mindful of this day's personal significance, the young person, along with parents and godparents should meet with clergy to review the intent of the rite, to select passages of Scripture, and to plan the service.

Hymns and readings for this service may be chosen from the list in the Rite of Passage for Young People and their Parents, or from the list on pages 34-36.

A homily may be preached, or, alternatively, parents, godparents, and friends of the young person may speak of their memories, knowledge, and love of the person.

The Gathering and Greeting

As the rite begins, the young person enters the church with her/his parents and godparents. Other persons may join the procession.

Opening Acclamation

Presider	Blessed be the one, holy, and living God
People	Glory to God for ever and ever.

or

Presider	Blessed be God who has brought us to this day.
People	Blessed be the God of all our days.

Presider	Thanks be to Jesus who restores us to wholeness.
People	Thanks be to Jesus in whose death is our life.

Presider	Praise to the Spirit who calls us to service.
People	Praise to the Spirit who leads us in love.

We gather to celebrate our *sister N.*, to give thanks for *her* _____ years of life, and to seek God's blessing for all the years to come.

Presider
Let us pray.

O God, we offer joyful thanks for our *sister N.* You knit *her* together and wonderfully made *her* to love you so that she may serve and delight in you all *her* days. On this day we rejoice as *she* takes on new responsibilities among your people. We bless *her* and call *her* into a graceful maturing. May *she* discover your will for *her* life, trusting in its unfolding in peace; through Jesus Christ, alive with you and the Holy Spirit throughout all ages. *Amen.*

A Hymn of Praise may be sung.

The Ministry of the Word

Suggested readings are listed on pp. 34-36.

Parents and godparents may read the lessons.

The Homily

The Presentation and/or Examination

The young person may be presented to the congregation by parents, godparents, or other sponsors with these or similar words.

I present *N.,* who comes to give thanks to God for *her* life, to commit *her* life to Christ, and to ask for the Holy Spirit's continued guidance in *her* life.

The following questions for parents and godparents may be used.

Presider	How has *N.* been faithful to her life in God?
Parents and Godparents	
	She has worshiped, prayed, and served in *her* community of faith.

Presider	How has *N.* been faithful to *her* life with others?
Parent and Godparents	
	She has been a true friend, a diligent student, and an active member of *her* family.

Presider	How has *N.* been faithful to herself?
Parents and Godparents	
	She is honest, forgiving, and kind. *She* is a delight to our hearts and we are proud of who *she* is and who *she* is becoming.

The Prayers

These Prayers for the Candidate at baptism in The Book of Common Prayer may be used, with this introduction and concluding collect in place of those in the Prayer Book

Let us pray for this young person who seeks God's blessing and ours as *she* journeys into adulthood.

Leader	Deliver her, O Lord, from the way of sin and death.
People	Lord, hear our prayer.
Leader	Open her heart to your grace and truth.
People	Lord, hear our prayer.
Leader	Fill her with your holy and life-giving Spirit.
People	Lord, hear our prayer.
Leader	Keep her in the faith and communion of your holy Church.
People	Lord, hear our prayer.
Leader	Teach her to love others in the power of the Spirit.
People	Lord, hear our prayer.
Leader	Send her into the world in witness to your love.
People	Lord, hear our prayer.
Leader	Bring her to the fullness of your peace and glory.
People	Lord, hear our prayer.

Grant, O Lord, that this young person, who is baptized into the death of Jesus Christ your Son, may continue *her* earthly journey in the power of his resurrection, and may wait in hope for his coming again in glory, who lives and reigns now and for ever. *Amen.*

In place of these prayers, others may be written for the occasion.

The Commitment of the Young Person
The young person may offer a personal prayer of thanksgiving and dedication composed for this occasion, or may bring a gift or symbol of thanksgiving to the altar or another appropriate devotional place.

The Blessing of the Young Person
The Presider, Parents, and Godparents may gather around and lay hands upon the young person as this prayer is offered.

Bless this child, O Lord, and sustain *her* in grace as *she* grows into maturity. As we prayed at *her* baptism, we continue to ask you to give *her* a questioning and discerning heart, a will that is brave and strong, a spirit knowing and loving the God who made *her*. May *she* delight in all your works as *she* continues to become the person you created *her* to be. Give *her* grace to speak forthrightly in truth. Let *her* greet new experiences with courage and hope. Help *her* discover true love. May *she* discern a calling that uses the gifts you have given *her*. Keep *her* safe and strong. Grant *her* health in old age. We pray especially that *she* may blossom in the knowledge that *she* is precious in your sight and in ours. Bless this child, O Lord, and sustain *her* in grace, in the name of *her* most faithful companion on the way, Jesus our Savior and Lord. *Amen.*

The Peace

The Eucharist

This Preface may be used at the Eucharist.

From day to day, from age to age, throughout our lives in this world and the next, you show yourself to be eternal Love, giver and sustainer of all goodness and joy; and so, with all the saints of every generation who are ancient in faith and young in hope, we join to sing your praise:

Suggested Readings

Ecclesiastes 11:7–9	(On youth, and the fear of God)
Isaiah 7:10–14	(A virgin is chosen by God)
Jeremiah 1:4–10	(The calling of Jeremiah)
1 Samuel 3:1–10	(The calling of Samuel)
Joel 2:28c–29	(I will pour out my Spirit)
Isaiah 61:1–11	(The Spirit of the Lord God is upon me)
Micah 6:6–8	(Do justice, love mercy, walk humbly with God)
Psalm 116	(God is our refuge)
Psalm 121	(My help comes from the Lord)
Psalm 144:12–15	(Prosperity for the people of God)

Canticles from *Enriching Our Worship 1*:

Canticle B
A Song of Pilgrimage *Priusquam errarem*
Ecclesiasticus 51:13-16, 20b-22

Before I ventured forth,
even while I was very young, *
  I sought wisdom openly in my prayer.
In the forecourts of the temple I asked for her, *
  and I will seek her to the end.
From first blossom to early fruit, *
  she has been the delight of my heart.
My foot has kept firmly to the true path, *
  diligently from my youth have I pursued her.
I inclined my ear a little and received her; *

I found for myself much wisdom and became adept in her.
To the one who gives me wisdom will I give glory, *
    for I have resolved to live according to her way.
From the beginning I gained courage from her, *
    therefore I will not be forsaken.
In my inmost being I have been stirred to seek her, *
    therefore have I gained a good possession.
As my reward the Almighty has given me the gift of language,*
    and with it will I offer praise to God.

Canticle K
A Song of Our Adoption
Ephesians 1:3-10

Blessed are you, the God and Father of our Lord Jesus Christ, *
    for you have blessed us in Christ
    with every spiritual blessing in the heavenly places.
Before the world was made, you chose us to be yours in Christ, *
    that we should be holy and blameless before you.
You destined us for adoption as your children through Jesus Christ,*
    according to the good pleasure of your will,
To the praise of your glorious grace, *
    that you have freely given us in the Beloved.
In you, we have redemption through the blood of Christ,
    the forgiveness of our sins,
According to the riches of your grace *
    which you have lavished upon us.
You have made known to us, in all wisdom and insight, *
    the mystery of your will,
According to your good pleasure which you set forth in Christ, *
    as a plan for the fullness of time,
To gather together all things in Christ, *
    things in heaven and things on earth.

Galatians 3:27–29	(In Christ there is no male or female)
Galatians 4:4–7	(We are sons and daughters of the same God)
Ephesians 1:3–6	(God chose us in Christ before creation)
1 John 4:7–11	(Beloved, let us love one another)
Romans 12:1–8	(Present your bodies as a living sacrifice)
Matthew 25:1–13	(The parable of wise and foolish virgins)
Luke 1:26–38	(The Annunciation of Gabriel to Mary)
Luke 1:46–55	(The Magnificat)
Luke 2:41–51	(The boy Jesus at the temple)

Other suggestions for readings:

• The Proper for the Saint whose name the young person shares
• The Proper for the Saint whose feast falls on the young person's birthday
• Readings selected according to the meaning of the young person's name, e.g., Lucy/light, Angelica/angels.

The Blessing of a Betrothal

Note: This rite has been designed specifically for use within the Episcopal Church, and the Declaration of Intention is a legally required document for couples married within the Episcopal Church. Use of this rite in other churches may require the rewording or omission of the Declaration of Intention.

The couple gather in the church or other suitable place with family, friends, and members of the congregation.

If the rite is celebrated at the Sunday Eucharist, the Ministry of the Word is celebrated in the usual manner, with the proper appointed for the Sunday. The Prayers of the People include intercession for the couple among the concerns of the local community. The Blessing of a Betrothal takes place immediately after the Prayers of the People, and the rite is followed immediately by the Peace.

If the rite is not celebrated at the Sunday Eucharist, it begins as follows

Presider	Blessed be God who has brought us to this day.
People	Blessed be the God of all our days.
Presider	Thanks be to Jesus who restores us to wholeness.
People	Thanks be to Jesus in whose death is our life.
Presider	Praise to the Spirit who calls us to service.
People	Praise to the Spirit who leads us in love.

A hymn, psalm, or suitable song may be sung.

One or more passages of Scripture selected by the couple may be read. If there is to be a Communion, a passage from the Gospel always concludes the readings. Suitable passages include

Ruth 1:16b–17a
Song of Solomon 2:1–3a, 4

Psalm 100
Psalm 117

Romans 13:9–13
1 John 4:7–8
John 15:9–12

The Presider then addresses the People in these or similar words

Dear friends: *N.N.* and *N.N.* have come asking our witness and prayers as they publicly declare their intention to marry [on ___]. In this time of betrothal, they have entrusted themselves to one another, and all are called to respect the bounds of their relationship. I invite *N.* and *N.* to come forward now, that we may hear their promises to one another.

The couple stand before the Presider, who asks them
Is either of you now promised to another?

The man and woman respond together
I am not.

The Presider turns to the woman and says
N., is it your will and intention to marry this man, N., who stands here before you?

The woman responds
It is.

The Presider says to the man
N., is it your will and intention to marry this woman, N., who stands here before you?

The man responds
It is.

Here the couple may read aloud and then sign the following Declaration of Intention (from Canon I.18 of the Canons of the Episcopal Church). If they do not sign the Declaration at this time, they shall do so in the context of their canonically required instruction as to the nature, meaning, and purpose of Holy Matrimony.

We, *A. B.* and *C. D.*, desiring to receive the blessing of Holy Matrimony in the Church, do solemnly declare that we hold marriage to be a lifelong union of husband and wife as it is set forth in the Book of Common Prayer. We believe that the union of husband and wife, in heart, body, and mind, is intended by God for their mutual joy; for the help and comfort given one another in prosperity and adversity; and, when it is God's will, for the procreation of children and their nurture in the knowledge and love of the Lord. And we do engage ourselves, so far as in us lies, to make our utmost effort to establish this relationship and to seek God's help thereto.

The Presider asks the people
Will you recognize this couple, and support and pray for them during this time of engagement?

The People respond
We will.

If an engagement ring has already been presented, the Presider takes the woman's left hand and blesses that ring, using the prayer of blessing below. When desired, a mutual exchange of rings may be made, or some other suitable symbol of commitment may be used in place of the engagement ring(s). If a ring or other symbol is to be given during this service, the Presider first says these or similar words

From of old, the chief sign of betrothal has been the giving and receiving of a ring. *N.*, is it your intention to give *N.* a ring as a symbol of your commitment?

The man responds
It is.

The man places an engagement ring on the left hand of the woman.

The Presider then blesses the ring (or other symbol) in these or similar words
Loving God, sanctify this sign of the intention of *N.* and *N.* to be joined together in holy matrimony. Bless and sustain them in their commitment to each other, that they may return before you to fulfill this solemn pledge, through Jesus Christ, in the power of the Holy Spirit. *Amen.*

The Presider continues
Let us pray for *N.* and *N.* and the pledge they have made.

Silence

Blessed are you, Lord our God. You give abundant joy to *N.* and *N.* Pour out your grace upon them, and bring them to the day of their wedding in safety and peace. We pray in the name of Christ our Savior. *Amen.*

The Presider says to the couple
Greet each other with a holy kiss.

The couple greet each other, after which the Peace may be exchanged throughout the congregation. When communion is to follow, the liturgy continues with the Offertory, at which the couple may present the offerings of bread and wine.

Preface of the Season

⌘

Prayers and a Rite for
the Transitions of Midlife

⌘

THE PRAYERS

1. Beginning a New Job

Holy God, you call us to do the works of Christ who came to live among us in love as a servant. Our true call is to be transformed into his likeness. As *N.* begins this new job, grant *him* wisdom and skill, so that the work of *his* hands may bring *him* satisfaction. Help *him* to be faithful, honest, and fair with those who labor beside *him,* and let them be so with *him.* May *he* glorify you in all *he* does, through Christ whose saving work on the cross brings us to rest in your love. *Amen.*

2. Ending a Job

Author of Life, you ordered the seasons and watch over the times between sowing and reaping, fallow and planting. We pray with *N.,* whose work in this place has now ended. During *her years* at this job, *she* faithfully accomplished *her* tasks, befriending those who worked beside *her.* Bless *her* as *she* leaves [and enters a period of waiting]. Bring relief if *she* is anxious. Strengthen *her* trust in you, [and guide *her* search for new work]. By the power of the Holy Spirit, assure *her* of your continuing love and care, and of *her* usefulness in the work of your kingdom; through Christ the Worker, our ever present help and companion. *Amen.*

3. Earning a GED (General Equivalency Diploma) or Other Diploma

Gracious God, you are always calling us to stretch our hearts in love and stretch our minds in learning. Through patience and perseverance, our *brother N.* has earned *his GED.* We thank you for your gifts of courage, determination, discipline which have kept *him* committed to *his* goal, and brought *him* to this proud day. As *he* faces life's next challenge, renew *him* in your love, and strengthen *him* to do your will; through Christ our Lord. *Amen.*

4. Release from Prison

Liberating God, we lose our true freedom when we wander from your love, but when we come home to you, we receive fullness of joy. Our *sister N.* ends *her prison/jail* sentence and returns to a world that waits for *her.* Calm *her* fears and guard *her* from stumbling; surround *her* with friendship, and fill *her* with hope, reassured by your love and ours; through Jesus your Christ, our Redeemer and Liberator. *Amen.*

5. Returning to a Community of Faith

Holy One, in Israel's pilgrimage through the wilderness you gathered a People of God. Our *brother N.* has traveled far from this community but never out of your sight or our hearts. We thank you for the care and love *he* received in *his* journey, and for lighting *his* path back to us. Bless our reunion with joy as we celebrate *his* return. We ask this in the name of Jesus, who is our path, our destination, and our companion on the way. *Amen.*

6. Surviving a Tragedy

Loving Father, you comfort us in times of affliction: Our *sister N.* has suffered a great tragedy and needs your healing. Send your Holy Spirit to soothe the anger, fear, and sorrow of *her* broken heart. In the darkness of this moment, shine the light of your radiant love. Be *her* companion in *her* grief. In *her* pain, make *her* strong in courage, dry *her* tears, mend *her* heart, and gently call *her* to newness of life. We thank you for the assurance of your love, shown in your Son Jesus, who suffered for us, died, and rose again to prepare our place in your eternal home. *Amen.*

7. At the Ending of a Relationship

God of Love, you ask us in your name to be faithful to the covenants we create with one another. Yet the relationship between *N.* and *N.* seems damaged beyond repair. We grieve with them as they say farewell to set off on separate paths, sorrowing for a love broken beyond our power to make it whole again. But you in your mercy rise in every death, and your love is new every morning. Help us to uphold *N.* and *N.* as they discern the future you hold in store for them: abundance of life in the love of Jesus Christ our Lord. *Amen.*

8. Healing after a Divorce

Holy One, in the bond of marriage you provide a sign of your eternal love for us. When our love is strong and true, we feel cradled in your embrace; when love breaks, we feel lost to you. Yet you are the God who holds your people in a sacred covenant, loving each of us as though there were but one of us. The marriage of *N.* and *N.* has ended, and so we seek your healing for their hearts and lives. Help them forgive whatever wounds they inflicted on each other. Let them surrender their past, looking with hope toward the future you bring them. Guard and heal *their children and* those who grieve their parting from one another. And bring us all to that day when our love will be made perfect and our joy complete in you, through Jesus Christ, in whom all things find perfection. *Amen.*

9. Renewing our Stewardship of Creation

Creator of all, we come to a time in our lives where we are filled with the understanding that we are part of all you have made. We thank you for the variety of your creation. Its complexity fills us with wonder and stretches our imaginations. Make yourself known to us as we strive to be good stewards of our environment, for as you placed Adam in a garden in Eden, you have set us in this world to help it flourish and live in harmony and peace with all living things. We acknowledge our past sins against creation with sorrow. Rekindle your light shining through us, so that we may know the work you have given us on this earth and declare your glory; through Jesus Christ, who with you and the Holy Spirit, upholds your creation through all ages. *Amen.*

10. Taking on the Care of Elder Parents

In the circle of life, O Gracious One, your signs of love shine out in every situation, through dying and rebirth, growing up and growing old, holding on and letting go. Now *N., N., N.,* will be looking after their parent(s), *N.,* [*and N*]. Those who gave care now need to receive care; those who once were supported by them now need be supporters. We pray this family may gracefully accept these changes. Grant them wisdom, good humor, patience and hope, as life continues according to your constant love, and bless their days with wellness, safety, and peace; through Christ our Redeemer. *Amen.*

11. Reclaiming Health

Holy One of Blessing: Your desire for your people is wholeness and health, and in our afflictions you draw near us with compassion. You whisper love to our hearts in pain, sorrow and fear; you fill our spirits with hope and heal our bodies. You have sustained our *brother N.*, O Lord, through *his* illness. You were *his* light in the darkness; in the valley of shadows, you stood with *him*, helping *him* to know you more deeply than before. May *he* enjoy renewed health and find *his* place at your banqueting table, joyfully taking up the work to which *he* is called, and for which *he* is given the gifts of your Spirit. We pray this in the name of Christ the Good Shepherd. *Amen.*

12. Beginning or Resuming a Dating Relationship

Our greatest joy in life, O God, is to love. We thank you for showing us through Jesus that loving one another makes us more fully human, created in your image. As *N.* stands ready to begin (resume) dating, help *her* to remember that love is sacred. May *she* bring to each new date hope for a true friendship. May *she* listen, and speak, and act with the greatest respect for *herself* and *her* companion. May *she* strive for a relationship that is truthful, patient, courageous, and kind. Above all, may love teach *her* to love you more and more as, through the Spirit's care, *she* grows in the image of Jesus Christ our Redeemer. *Amen.*

Receiving or Claiming a New Name

In many cultures the giving or the taking of a new name signifies and empowers a radical change in the life of the individual and has great significance in the whole community: some examples might be a woman after a divorce reclaiming the surname she was born with or a child taking the name of his adopted parents. When an event or experience leads a member to take or be given a new name, the following may be used to mark this transition in the parish community.

The Gathering and Greeting

The Gathering Rite may reflect the particular culture celebrating this new name. It may include such elements as ritual cleansing, confession, incense or smudging, singing, and drumming. It concludes with this Collect:

Holy One of Blessing, in baptism you bring us to new life in Jesus Christ and you name us Beloved. We give you thanks for the renewal of that life and love in *N.*, who now takes on (*or chooses*) a new name. Strengthen and uphold *him* as *he* grows into the power, and authority, and meaning of this name; we pray in the Name above all names, Jesus, your Son, whom with you and the Holy Spirit, the Triune God, we adore. *Amen.*

The Liturgy of the Word

The Proper for the Feast of the Holy Name (January 1) may be used: Exodus 34:1-8; Psalm 8; Romans 1:1-7 or Philippians 2:9-13; Luke 2:15-21. Other readings appropriate to the occasion may be used. A homily may be preached, or, alternatively, the candidate may share the journey and experiences that resulted in this new name, inviting the community's assistance in living into its significance

The Prayers of the People

Leader

We pray for the Church you love as a spouse; may it faithfully bear Christ's name in its communion and work. Remembering its ministers, and all the baptized, especially those we name before you:

The People add their particular intercessions.

Leader

We pray for the world you created; may its people, together, call themselves family, and all nations come to your peace. Remembering nations at war and in danger, especially we name before you:

The People add their particular intercessions.

Leader

We pray for the afflicted; may they find healing and hope, and help in their sorrows. Remembering all who suffer, especially we name before you:

The People add their particular intercessions.

Leader

We pray for all the departed; may they grow more and more in likeness to you. Remembering all the saints, especially we name before you:

The People add their particular intercessions.

Leader

We pray for your servant *N.*, with thanks for the journey and awakening that have brought *him* to this moment, for *his* place amongst your people, and for *his* gifts and calling to serve you.

The Presider concludes with this collect:

O God, in renaming your servants Abraham, Sarah, Jacob, Peter, and Paul, you gave them new lives and new tasks, new love and new hope. We now hold before you our companion, *N.* Bless *him* with a new measure of grace as *he* takes this new name. Write *him* again in your heart and on your palm. And grant that we all may be worthy to call ourselves Christian, for the sake of your Christ whose name is Love, and in whom, with you and the Spirit, we pray. *Amen.*

The Giving of the Name

The new name is given.
The following forms may be used.

Presider	By what name shall *N.* be known?
Sponsor	The name shall be *N.*
Candidate	My name is *N.*

or

Presider	By what name shall you be known?
Candidate	My name shall be *N.*
Presider	Your name shall be *N.*

The community may respond by repeating
Your name shall be *N.*

Presider   Bear this name in the Name of Christ. Share it in the name of mercy. Offer it in the name of justice.

The candidate may offer gifts that symbolize this change. Members of the community may present the candidate with symbolic gifts.

The Peace

During the exchange of the Peace each member of the community may address the candidate by the new name.

N., the Peace of Christ be with you.

The Eucharist

In the place of the usual postcommunion prayer the following may be used.

Gracious God, you have fed us heavenly food in the sacrament of the body and blood of Christ. Grant that with N. (*new name*), we may share in this mystery and may, with *him*, ever turn to the One whose Name is above all names, our Lord and Savior, Jesus Christ. *Amen.*

Blessing and Dismissal

⌘

Prayers and Rites for the Transitions of Elders

⌘

THE PRAYERS

1. Retiring

To everything, Lord, you have given a season, calling each thing good in its time. In the years of our lives, you call us to work, you ask us to play, you command us to rest, and by your grace, you weave our days together in peace. We pray for our *brother N.*, who comes to the end of *his* season of work. Thank you for friends made, challenges met, and growth enjoyed, and for all *he* has learned and accomplished. Help *him* now let the old work go, to take up the new life for which you have also given *him* gifts; through Christ the Worker, in whose love is our eternal rest and joy. *Amen.*

2. Celebrating a Wedding Anniversary

You unite your people in marriage, O God, delighting in us as the joyful bride of your heart. In the union of *N.* and *N.*, we remember your faithfulness, and the tender love in which you hold and behold us for ever. Calling them together, you have helped them make their love a strong rock on which they have built a sacred companionship. You have granted them moments and days and now _____ years of blessedness. We rejoice in their contentment, promising to support and honor them. We ask that our own loves may display the constancy of theirs. Protect them this day and always, as together they grow in your likeness and grace; through Christ who blessed the wedding feast at Cana. *Amen.*

3. Becoming a Grandparent or Great-Grandparent

Your love, O God, is fresh as an infant's, playful as a child's.
Your love, O God, contains the hopefulness of youth and the watchfulness of age.
Your love, O God, is fierce as a mother's, steady as a father's, loving and wise,
O Eldest of elders.

Your love, O God, is present in the love of *N. and N.,* who, through the *birth/adoption* of [*name of child*], have become [great-] grandparents. What joys in life compare to this? Let us share in their joy. Instruct their hearts in that love you hand down from generation to generation, from parents through children's children and to every age. Grant them many years, and descendents as countless as the stars, and bring us all together, at length, to the heavenly banquet laid by Jesus, your Christ and our Savior. *Amen.*

Farewell to a Home

Often, elders move from the larger house in which their children were raised to a smaller house or apartment, or find themselves in need of assisted living. Members of a community may wish to support the elder(s) during this transition.

In preparation for the rite, a candle may be lighted in each room, and left burning until the procession is departing from that room.

The Elder(s) and the People pray

Gracious God, your heart is our eternal home, and your love is as present in sorrow as in joy; our *sister N.* is prepared to depart from this house. Help *her* carry the moments of grace *she* has known here to *her* new home.

The Elder and her *companions may travel through the rooms of the house, recalling memories and naming feelings evoked by each room.*

As the group leaves the room, the Elder(s) extinguish the light, saying

With thanks for my time in it, I leave this room to those who will dwell in this place, asking joy for their days and peace for their nights.

At the end of the procession, the People may pray

Sojourning God, you go before *N.* (and *N.*) preparing the way to a peaceful new home. Give *her* grace to let go of the old, accepting the comfort and assistance of those around *her*. Help *her* know that you are as near as *her* breath; let *her* hear your whisper of the undying love in which you hold *her* as you held *her* in the beginning. We pray this through Christ our Savior. *Amen.*

A Celebration of Life on the Occasion of a Significant Birthday

The Gathering and Greeting

Gathering Music

The Elder(s), with his presenters, join the procession, and are seated at the front of the assembly.

Salutation

Presider	Blessed be the one, holy, and living God.
People	Glory to God for ever and ever.

or

Presider	Blessed be God who has brought us to this day.
People	Blessed be the God of all our days.

Presider	Thanks be to Jesus who restores us to wholeness.
People	Thanks be to Jesus in whose death is our life.

Presider	Praise to the Spirit who calls us to service.
People	Praise to the Spirit who leads us in love.

The Collect

Presider	The Lord be with you.
People	And also with you.
Presider	Let us pray.

God of Wisdom, your love is ageless, and you remain faithful through every breath of our lives. All creation has been formed for the fullness of your eternal joy. Give us grace to shine with that goodness and hope which is your blessing, and through your Spirit to continue in Christ, in whom we gather and pray, this day and always. *Amen.*

The Ministry of the Word

Suggested Readings are listed on p. 58-60.

The Presentation

Presider   On the occasion of *his* _____ birthday, we gather around *N.*, who comes before God and this faithful community to give thanks for the gift of life and to ask God's blessing on all *his* days to come. Let the community now present *him.*

Family and friends gather around the Presider and Elder. Each person presents the Elder, with such phrases as

- I present *N.*, my *husband*, who has lived with me in the covenant of marriage, showing me God's faithful love.

- *I/we* present *N.*, *my/our mother*, who has shown *me/us* God's firm and gentle love.

- *I/we* present *N.*, *my/our father*, who has guarded *me/us* in the strength of God's watchful love.

- *I/we* present *N.*, *my/our grandmother*, who has lavished *me/us* with God's unconditional love.

- I present *N.*, my friend of _____ years, whose love has been constant and true.

- I present *N.*, my *uncle*, whose love is knowing, playful, and wise.

Or the Elder(s) may simply be presented.

We present *N.* (*N., N.,*).

The Thanksgiving and Dedication of the Elder(s)

The Elder(s)

I give thanks to the Lord of Life for this and all my days, and I seek God's help for the life that remains. I am richly blessed by you, my family and friends, and thankful that I belong among the people of God. Therefore, I promise before God and you to continue to serve Christ faithfully in worship and prayer, by repentance and by forgiving others, by seeking Christ in the midst of suffering, and by working for justice and peace. In these latter years of my earthly pilgrimage, I will remain near you, blessing each day you give me, and seeking abundance of life to which we all are called. For these things, I ask God's help and your prayers and love.

or

I thank the Lord of Life for you, my *family and friends* who have blessed my life. Stay with me through whatever lies before us. May you and I continue to worship and pray together and ask forgiveness when we have wronged one another. Let us work together for justice and peace in the midst of a suffering world. For the rest of my time with you, help me be thankful for each day as it is given, remembering that God gives us abundant life. For these gifts I ask your prayers, your help, and your love.

The Prayers for the Elder(s)

Leader

Holy One of Life and Love: Hear your People as we pray. For the Church of your Christ; for all its ministers; for vision, calling, and mission; for courage, in all its members, to love and to serve, we are asking you, O God

Hear your People as we pray.

For this community of ____: for its pastors and people; for truth and tenderness among its members; for the will to create a bright future; for passion to befriend the needy and poor, we are asking you, O God

Hear your People as we pray.

For the world you created and love: for peace among nations; for an end to war; for the victims of famine and flood; for [*the People may be invited to name particular concerns for the world*]; we are asking you, O God

Hear your People as we pray.

For all who suffer: for relief from pain and fear; for assurance of your nearness; for healing of hurts; for hope and strength; [and for *N., N., N*]; we are asking you, O God

Hear your People as we pray.

For all the departed: for their continued growth in grace and love; for the witness of the lives they shared with us; for their eternal rest in the land of light and joy; for *N., N., N.*; we are asking you, O God

Hear your People as we pray.

For our beloved *N.* (*N., N.*): for comfort in *his* sorrows, losses, and fears; for strength in *his* frailties and healing of *his* heartaches; for the discernment of new ways to serve; for grace in all the days to come; assuring *him* of our thanksgiving and love, we are asking you, O God

Hear your People as we pray.

For all whom we love and all who love us; for the gifts of the Spirit flowing through us; for the hope of Jesus' resurrection in our lives

Be our Help and Companion, we are asking you, O God,
and hear your People as we pray. Amen.

Tributes and Gifts

The People may address the Elder(s)

N., N., we give thanks for the gift of your wisdom, the fruit of your years. We thank you for keeping alive the memories, stories, and traditions you pass on to us in this congregation. We learn from the wealth of your experience. We promise to stay with you through the end of your days among us, and to hold you in our hearts and memories, whatever lies ahead. We will listen to you, grieve with your losses, and pray with you through times of trial. We will encounter Christ in you as you continue to serve in his Name. Reflect Christ's wisdom and grace in our midst, and now receive these gifts as signs of our love.

Representatives of groups that have been important in the life of the Elder(s) may come forward and offer a tribute in thanksgiving to God and in honor of the person. Greetings representing the Elder's passion, dedication, interest or skill may be offered.

N., receive this _____, as a sign of _____.

The Blessing of the Elder(s)

May God, our Creator, transform you in love, every day, for all time. *Amen.*

May Christ our Savior keep your soul in life, and lead you to the joys of heaven. *Amen.*

May the Holy Spirit, our Companion,
  surround you and hold you in peace all your days. *Amen.*

And may the blessing of God, Triune and Holy, be upon you and among us,
  this day and forever. *Amen.*

Suggested Readings

Proverbs 2:1–11	(The Lord gives wisdom; from his mouth come wisdom and understanding.)
Proverbs 3:13–24	(Trust in the Lord with all your heart.)
Proverbs 8:1–21	(Does not wisdom call, and understanding raise her voice?)
Hosea 14:4–9	(I will be like the dew to Israel.)

Canticles from *Enriching Our Worship 1:*

Canticle A
A Song of Wisdom *Sapientia liberavit*
Wisdom 10:15-19, 20b-21

Wisdom freed from a nation of oppressors *
  a holy people and a blameless race.
She entered the soul of a servant of the Lord, *
  withstood dread rulers with wonders and signs.

To the saints she gave the reward of their labors, *
  and led them by a marvelous way;
She was their shelter by day *
  and a blaze of stars by night.

She brought them across the Red Sea, *
  she led them through mighty waters;
But their enemies she swallowed in the waves *
  and spewed them out from the depths of the abyss.

And then, Lord, the righteous sang hymns to your Name, *
  and praised with one voice your protecting hand;
For Wisdom opened the mouths of the mute, *
  and gave speech to the tongues of a new-born people.

Canticle B
A Song of Pilgrimage *Priusquam errarem*
Ecclesiasticus 51:13-16, 20b-22

Before I ventured forth,
even while I was very young, *
  I sought wisdom openly in my prayer.
In the forecourts of the temple I asked for her, *
  and I will seek her to the end.
From first blossom to early fruit, *
  she has been the delight of my heart.
My foot has kept firmly to the true path, *
  diligently from my youth have I pursued her.
I inclined my ear a little and received her; *
  I found for myself much wisdom and became adept in her.

To the one who gives me wisdom will I give glory, *
    for I have resolved to live according to her way.
From the beginning I gained courage from her, *
    therefore I will not be forsaken.
In my inmost being I have been stirred to seek her, *
    therefore have I gained a good possession.
As my reward the Almighty has given me the gift of language,*
    and with it will I offer praise to God.

1 Corinthians 1:20–30   (God's foolishness is wiser than human wisdom.)
1 Corinthians 12:4–13 (There are varieties of gifts, but the same Spirit.)
James 3:13–18   (Who is wise and understanding among you?)
1 Peter 5:1–7   (I exhort the elders among you)

Suggested Hymns and Spiritual Songs

Additional suggestions are listed on pp. 79-82.

From *The Hymnal 1982*

611	Christ, the worker
549, 550	Jesus calls us
482	Lord of all hopefulness
554	Tis the gift to be simple

From *Lift Every Voice and Sing II*

189	Great is thy faithfulness

From *Wonder, Love, and Praise*

747	God, the sculptor of the mountains
819	Guide my feet, Lord
757	Will you come and follow me

From other sources

I was there to hear your borning cry (Fortress Press)
Bless now, O God, this journey
Make me a channel of your peace (Oregon Catholic Press)
Bind us Together (Kingsway's Thank You Music)
Bring Many Names

A Rite for the Blessing or Commissioning of an Elder

This rite celebrates the special gifts for ministry some Elders possess. It welcomes one or more Elders into a ministry of wisdom and presence in the faithful community.

The Gathering and Greeting

Presider	We are gathered to celebrate *N.* [*these Elders*] who has blessed our lives and served the Christ through years of faithful discipleship, and who seeks, now, to serve the Church as an Elder in a ministry of leadership, counsel, wisdom, and grace.
People	Thanks be to God.
Presider	Let us ask the Holy Spirit to pour out upon us gifts for serving the world God loves.

The Collect

Presider	The Lord be with you.
People	And also with you.
Presider	Let us pray.

God of Wisdom, your love is ageless, and you remain faithful through every breath of our lives. All creation has been formed for the fullness of your eternal joy. Give us grace to shine with that goodness and hope which is your blessing, and through your Spirit to continue in Christ, in whom we gather and pray, this day and always. *Amen.*

The Ministry of the Word

Suggested Readings are listed on pp. 58-60.

A homily may be preached or, alternatively, children, colleagues, and friends of the Elder may speak of their memories, knowledge, and love of him or her.

The Examination

The Elder and his or her presenters gather in front of the assembly.

Presenters	We present *N.*, born (*date*), to be recognized as an Elder of this community.
Presider	Is *N.* faithful in ministry and in prayer?
Presenters	*She* is.
Presider	Is *N.* diligent in caring for *herself* and others?
Presenters	*She* is.

Presider	Does *N.* seek God's abundant grace on all life?
Presenters	*She* does.

Presider to Elder

Are you prepared to offer the gifts of your presence and wisdom to this community?

Elder	I am.
Presider	Are you willing to permit others to learn from their mistakes?
Elder	I am.
Presider	Will you continue to reflect the presence of Christ to this faithful community and to the world?
Elder	I will.

The Elder continues with these words of Commitment:

I give thanks to the Lord of Life for this and all my days, and I seek God's help for the life that remains. I am richly blessed by you, my family and friends, and thankful that I belong among the people of God. Therefore, I promise before God and you to continue to serve Christ faithfully in worship and prayer, by repentance and by forgiving others, by seeking Christ in the midst of suffering, and by working for justice and peace. In these latter years of my earthly pilgrimage, I will remain near you, blessing each day you give me, and seeking that abundance of life to which we all are called. For these things, I ask God's help and your prayers and love.

or this

With God's help, I will show Christ to you and to the world. I will care for you and accept your care for me, striving to speak the truth in love and holding us all in prayer. I will grow, learn, and serve at your side, helping to lead us in ever more faithful discipleship of the Lord of Life.

The Prayers of the People

Leader

In celebration of this and all our ministries, let us pray to the God of the Ages, saying, "Hear us, we pray."

Gracious One, we pray for the world you have made and love, so that its people might know you, and its beauty and goodness be preserved. God of the Ages

Hear us, we pray.

Gracious One, we pray for the Church, here and everywhere, gathered together in Christ, so that it may shine with his light, and humbly serve in his name. God of the Ages

Hear us, we pray.

Gracious One, we pray for all who suffer in sickness, in war, in heartache, and in loss, so that they might not despair of your help, which endures ever faithful, tender, and strong. God of the Ages

Hear us, we pray.

Gracious One, we pray for the departed, so that they might hold us before you as we always remember them, and grow in your likeness as they dwell in your love. God of the Ages

Hear us, we pray.

Gracious One, we pray for all children and youths, so that they might be nurtured and safe, following their hearts to your eternal life. God of the Ages

Hear us, we pray.

Gracious One, we pray for those in the middle of life, so that they might find strength in their work and joy in their rest. God of the Ages

Hear us, we pray.

Gracious One, we pray for N. and all our Elders who are living treasures and keepers of lore, so that they might be honored by us, held in your love, and remain ever faithful to the life you created. God of the Ages

Hear us, we pray.

Gracious One, Beloved God of all generations, we pray for ourselves that, one and all, we may be young in hope and ageless in wisdom. For our failures at love, forgive us. For the work of love, encourage us. For the gift of your unfailing compassion, make us thankful. As we near the end of our days, relieve our fear of death and make us bravely follow Jesus, who is Resurrection and Life, who takes away the sting and fear of death and gives life for all time, and in whose Name we pray. *Amen.*

Then, as hands are laid on the Elder, the Presider says

In the name of God and of this community, I recognize you as an Elder in this congregation and commission you to a ministry of presence and wisdom among us.

The newly commissioned Elder may pray over the community.

The Peace

If the service continues with the Eucharist, the following Preface may be used.

From day to day, from age to age, throughout our lives in this world and the next, you show yourself to be eternal Love, giver and sustainer of all goodness and joy; and so, with all the saints of every generation who are ancient in faith and young in hope, we join to sing your praise.

⊞

PRAYERS FOR
NATIONAL SERVICE

⊞

Prayers for National Service

Upon Entering Military Service

Almighty and everliving God, ruler of all things in heaven and on earth: Hear our prayers for *N.* as *he* enters military service. Be present with *him, his* family, and *his* community in this transition. Guide and govern *him* by your good Spirit. Protect *him* from evil, and lead us all into your peace; through Jesus Christ our Lord. *Amen.*

Upon Deployment

God our Rock and Refuge: We commend to your gracious care *N., N.,* and *N.,* who are being deployed in the service of our nation. Defend them day by day with your heavenly grace; strengthen them in their trials and temptations; give them courage to endure the perils which they may face; and grant that wherever they go, they may be assured of your abiding presence; through Christ our Savior. *Amen.*

For a Family Farewell to a Deployed Member

To be prayed by family members in church or at the place of parting
Into your hands, most merciful Savior,
we place our beloved *N.,*
asking you to be *his* tower of safety and strength,
his comfort and refuge in danger.
Watch over *him* wherever *he* goes.
Stand at *his* side in battle;
keep *him* safe from enemy and accident.
Defend *him*, waking and sleeping.
Bless *him* as he travels,
and let our love be an anchor and a joy for *him*
through the time we are apart;
and then, return *him* to us in safety.
We ask this in your holy Name. *Amen.*

For the Family Separated during Military Service

God, the fountain of all mercy, your love is made known to us in the love of others: Surround this family with the support and care of our community as they watch and wait for *N.'s* return; grant them patience, hope, and quiet confidence, until the time of reunion; through Christ we pray. *Amen.*

For Transfer or Change of Duty Station

Merciful God, be present with this community, and with *N., N.,* and *N.* [and their families] at their change of duty [transfer]. Guide and protect them in their new responsibilities. Surround us with your eternal presence as some go and others stay. In your Holy Name we pray. *Amen.*

Upon Return from Deployment

Almighty God, giver of every good gift, we praise and thank you for the return of *N.* from deployment. Be present as *he* strives to renew relationships and re-enter this community. Guide and guard *him* and us in this season of change. Wherever there is anxiety, pain, or hardship, bring healing through your grace and mercy. This we ask for your love's sake. *Amen.*

For Veterans

Lord our God, look favorably on [*N., N.,* and all] those who have served this nation in our armed forces. We thank you for your presence with them in their service. Help them and us to remember their fallen comrades, that the sacrifices we honor this day may never be forgotten. Let the light of liberty and the love of justice and mercy burn brightly in the heart of this nation, through Jesus Christ our Savior. *Amen.*

Upon Conscientious Objection to Military Service

Christ our Savior, Prince of Peace: Give to *N.* strength and courage to follow you in the path of nonviolence and embrace the disciplines of peace; for your mercy's sake. *Amen.*

For Alternative Service

Everliving God, in whom we live and move and have our being: be present with *N.* in *her* commitment to conscientious service, and lead and guide *her* in your ways. Grant this for the sake of Jesus Christ. *Amen.*

For National or Mission Service

Lord Christ, you came among us as one who served: Send your Holy Spirit to guide and strengthen *N.,* who is answering a call to service. Give *him* courage to persevere, and vision to see you present in all whom *he* serves; for you live and reign for ever and ever. *Amen.*

⊞

Prayers and a Rite
for Remembering the Departed

⊞

The service for the Burial of the Dead focuses on the bereaved, offering a public gathering in which to lament. It also opens the prospect of growth in the hope of resurrection. The first year after the death of a loved one is filled with many "first time without" experiences. Gatherings of friends and members of the church community may help mourners come to terms with the depth of their grief as they are reminded that Jesus Christ wept for the death of friends and feels our sorrows no less than our joys.

Certain moments in the church year affirm and rejoice in the communion of saints who guide and cheer us on in our journey toward heaven. Easter, All Saints' Day, and the Commemoration of All Faithful Departed (sometimes called All Souls' Day), along with certain national holidays such as Memorial Day, are all occasions for remembering departed loved ones. In addition, whenever the community gathers for Eucharist, we remember and pray for the departed who remain close to us, even while they now dwell in the greater presence of God. Our Christian faith assures us that death does not sever the bonds of love, but that our relationships live in faith and hope until the day when we will see God face to face in the presence of those we love who have gone before us.

Below are suggestions for remembering the departed, with collects for particular anniversaries marking the journey of grief's healing.

THE PRAYERS

1. A Week After a Death

2. A Month After a Death

3. A Year After a Death

4. Visiting the Site of a Death

5. Coming Home Without a Departed Loved One

6. Giving Away Belongings of a Departed Loved One

7. Visiting a Graveside

8. On the Birthday of a Departed Loved One

9. On Visiting the Site Where a Loved One was Last Encountered

10. On Grieving a Violent Death

11. Three Prayers for a Child Who Dies by Violence

1. A Week after a Death

God of our moments and hours, our days and our nights, we have lived a week without N. We would not have believed it could have been endured, yet here we are on a seventh day of mourning, hearts still breaking, tears still flowing, and still so in need of your help. Ease our sorrow, gracious God, as days flow into weeks, into months and years, until our courage grows strong again in the knowledge that even our darkest days are lit by your grace and love; through Christ, in the Spirit, we pray. *Amen.*

2. A Month after a Death

Gracious God, we have lived a month without N. Even in our deepest grief, the world has begun to fill the gaps left by *her* death. You have sent us consolation through the precious offerings of friends. Yet we continue to need your comfort and help in the work of mourning and healing. We commend N. to your care, as *she* grows daily in your presence. We pray through Jesus, your Christ, in whom we too look forward to the joys of heaven, and with whom in the Spirit we pray. *Amen.*

3. A Year after a Death

God of the living, you are the Way, the Truth and the Life: We have lived a year without N. Throughout that time of the turning earth, sun, and moon, you have shown us signs of your wonders: the Christmas star of Bethlehem, Easter's empty tomb, and the tongues of Pentecost fire, which speak of your glory and goodness to all creation. We have counted days of sorrow, laughter, and endurance in our journey through grief's stages. Now we can declare that even though we still feel bruised by the pain of our loss, life continues. You give us yourself in moments of grace, transforming us through your love. We thank you for the distance you have brought us during our year of healing, and ask you to help us become ever more whole in years to come. Keep N. present in our hearts, and may we honor *his* memory, embracing each new day with courage and faith; through Christ, in the Spirit, we pray. *Amen.*

4. Visiting the Site of a Death

Consoling God, this is the place where our *sister N.*, lost *her* life. Give us faith to see that *she* was not alone, for your love embraced *her* fear and pain as you took *her* home to you. This dreadful place became for her the gate of heaven where you welcomed your child into your eternal glory and rest; where you live and reign with Christ and the Holy Spirit for ever. *Amen.*

5. Coming Home Without a Departed Loved One

O God, here, in this dwelling, I have known the joys of home with *N.*, who will never return to this house. Help me live through my loss and grief, weeping every tear that needs to fall as I come to terms with the emptiness that *his* absence leaves. Give me a sense of our nearness as I sleep and wake, eat and rest, with a new sense of your nearness, knowing you fill this house and all our sorrows with your merciful presence and grace; through Christ whose heart is our eternal home, and with the Holy Spirit, Comforter and Guide. *Amen.*

6. Giving Away Belongings of a Departed Loved One

In the things of this world, O God, we taste and see and touch you in bread and wine, water and oil, where you make yourself known as Love. These possessions of our beloved *N.* remind us of *her* presence in our lives and hearts, and in this home. In letting go these objects which speak to us of *her* we open ourselves to you in our grief, remembering your words, "It is more blessed to give than to receive." We offer *her* up to you again as we give away *her* belongings, promising to wait in hope till we meet *her* in heaven's grace; through Christ, in whom there is joy for ever. *Amen.*

7. Visiting a Graveside

Thank you, God, for your good earth, which cradles the body of our beloved *N.*, and upholds our long journey through this world. Continue to meet us here, at this holy resting place, where earth and ashes and dust are returned to their source. Comfort us, always, in our sorrow and loss. Keep our feet planted in this world you created in your love, and turn our hearts and eyes to heaven, where our *brother* now lives with you in peace; through Christ our Lord. *Amen.*

8. The Birthday of a Departed Loved One

Gracious God, our days unfold according to your mercy. We remember our *sister N.* on her birthday, recalling *her* years among us. Thank you for having given *her* to us for that time, and help us rejoice in the knowledge that *she* lives with you now in the fullness of heaven's joy. May our hearts be bound to *her* continuing love for us as our hopes are bound to you. Strengthen our faith in expectation of that day when we, too, shall come to our eternal rest beside *her.* We pray in the name of the One in whose death we have our true life, your child Jesus Christ, who lives and reigns with you and the Holy Spirit, one God throughout all time. *Amen.*

9. On Visiting the Site Where a Loved One was Last Encountered

Holy and Merciful One, in this place I last saw *N.*, not realizing those would be our final moments together. Through the loss of my beloved, that occasion and this site have become hallowed to me.

Here the speaker may recall the occasion or ask forgiveness of God and the departed, silently or aloud.

Keep *N.* alive in my heart as I lift up my love and my memories of *her* to you. Help me recall that every moment in every place your Spirit hovers, comforting and guiding us to the shelter of the everlasting arms you stretch out to gather all your children in; through Christ our Lord. *Amen.*

10. On Grieving a Violent Death

Lord of Life, you trampled death under your feet so we might come alive in your eternal light. We remember before you our beloved *N.* In our anger and confusion, we need your help to find our way. When your own child, Jesus, suffered violent death, you acted through it to redeem the world. Help us live into that knowledge as we remember that *N.* now lives because of that great gift of your love. Help us release *him* to you. Show us that your hand has dried *his* tears, and let us glimpse his joy in your face. Grant us strength and the spirit of healing and peace so that we may labor for your just and peaceable kingdom, where all your children live in safety and fulfillment, through Jesus Christ our Lord. *Amen.*

11. For a Child who Dies by Violence

The prayers that follow are taken from "Burial of a Child" in Enriching Our Worship 2, © 2000 *by The Church Pension Fund. Used by permission.*

Loving God, Jesus gathered your little ones in his arms and blessed them. Have pity on those who mourn for *N.*, an innocent slaughtered by the violence of our fallen world. Be with us as we struggle with the mysteries of life and death; in our pain, bring your comfort, and in our sorrow, bring your hope and your promise of new life, in the name of Jesus our Savior. *Amen.*

or this

God our deliverer, gather our horror and pity for the death of your child *N.* into the compass of your wisdom and strength, that through the night we may seek and do what is right, and when morning comes trust ourselves to your cleansing justice and new life; through Christ our Savior. *Amen.*

or this

God, do not hide your face from us in our anger and grief for the death of *N.* Renew us in hope that your justice will roll down like mighty waters and joy spring up from the broken ground in a living stream; through Jesus our Savior. *Amen.*

REMEMBERING A DEPARTED SOUL

A celebration of the Holy Eucharist, by remembering the departed, also reminds the congregation of the heavenly banquet Jesus prepares for us in eternity.

The Gathering
Songs, hymns, or one or more of these anthems that begin The Burial of the Dead in The Book of Common Prayer may be used.

I am Resurrection and I am Life, says the Lord.
Whoever has faith in me shall have life,
even though he die.
And everyone who has life,
and has committed himself to me in faith,
shall not die for ever.

As for me, I know that my Redeemer lives
and that at the last he will stand upon the earth.
After my awaking, he will raise me up;
and in my body I shall see God.
I myself shall see, and my eyes behold him
who is my friend and not a stranger.

For none of us has life in himself,
and none becomes his own master when he dies.
For if we have life, we are alive in the Lord,
and if we die, we die in the Lord.
So, then, whether we live or die,
we are the Lord's possession.

Happy from now on
are those who die in the Lord!
So it is, says the Spirit,
for they rest from their labors.

In the midst of life we are in death;
from whom can we seek help?
From you alone, O Lord,
who by our sins are justly angered.

Holy God, Holy and Mighty,
Holy and merciful Savior,
deliver us not into the bitterness of eternal death.

Lord, you know the secrets of our hearts;
shut not your ears to our prayers,
but spare us, O Lord.

Holy God, Holy and Mighty,
Holy and merciful Savior,
deliver us not into the bitterness of eternal death.

O worthy and eternal Judge,
do not let the pains of death
turn us away from you at our last hour.

Holy God, Holy and Mighty,
Holy and merciful Savior,
deliver us not into the bitterness of eternal death.

The Greeting

The Presider may welcome the people by explaining the purpose of the gathering.

The Collect

An appropriate Collect from the Prayers for Remembering the Departed may be used, or from
The Burial of the Dead in The Book of Common Prayer, or the Commemoration of All Faithful
Departed (sometimes called All Souls Day) in Lesser Feasts and Fasts.

The Liturgy of the Word

Lessons may be chosen from The Burial of the Dead in The Book of Common Prayer, or from the
following, which address ongoing grief:

Isaiah 35:1–10
Psalm 13
Psalm 31:9–10, 14–16
1 Thessalonians 4:13–18

In addition to the readings from Scripture, other writings and poems may be offered.

A homily may follow, and worshipers may speak of their memories of the departed loved one.

The Apostles' Creed

I believe in God, the Father almighty,
    creator of heaven and earth.
I believe in Jesus Christ, his only Son, our Lord.
    He was conceived by the power of the Holy Spirit
        and born of the Virgin Mary.
    He suffered under Pontius Pilate,
        was crucified, died, and was buried.
    He descended to the dead.
    On the third day he rose again.
    He ascended into heaven,
        and is seated at the right hand of the Father.
    He will come again to judge the living and the dead.
I believe in the Holy Spirit,
    the holy catholic Church,
    the communion of saints,
    the forgiveness of sins,
    the resurrection of the body,
    and the life everlasting. Amen.

The Prayers of the People

A form for the prayers may be taken from The Book of Common Prayer, or the following form may be used.

Lord Jesus Christ, you are Resurrection and Life: Hear our prayers on behalf of our *brother, N.*; (for *N. and N.*), for this whole community, and all who continue to mourn *his* departing. Even as we grieve, we also give thanks for the fullness of joy in which *he* lives with you now, and toward which we faithfully travel in healing and hope. We speak *N.'s* name in assurance of *his* eternal life with you, and ask your healing help for our wounded hearts.

We pray to you, Jesus.

We thank you for the way *he* lived, and for the love *he* gave us, rejoicing in the knowledge that *he* has returned to your paradise where there is no sorrow or sighing, but eternal joy in your presence.

We pray to you, Jesus.

We lay our grief before you, for you also grieved at the grave of your friend, Lazarus. Give us courage to open our hearts to others, and to weep tears that still need to fall.

We pray to you, Jesus.

We thank you for all relationships, for those whose love brings us joy; help us testify to your presence in this broken world.

We pray to you, Jesus.

We ask you to help us live our faith, to take up our work, to correct our course when we stray from you, to give and forgive, and to seek your face in all that we do, so that when we, too, come to die, we will surely have known the fullness of life.

We pray to you, Jesus.

We thank you, Jesus, for those who have gone before us. Through their lives you helped us learn that in every season of life and death you are near us, standing firm when we falter. We long for the time when your own hand will dry all our tears. Be our Companion this day, our path on the way, and our door to life eternal, as we place ourselves in your love, O Christ, who, with our Father and the Holy Spirit, live in glory everlasting. *Amen.*

APPENDIX

Suggested Music for Rites of Passage
From *The Hymnal 1982*

8	Morning has broken
9	Not here for high and holy things (especially vv 4–6)
33, 34, 35	Christ mighty Savior (especially for passages of older people)
370	I bind unto myself today
396, 397	Now thank we all our God
400	All creatures of our God and king
408	Sing praise to God who reigns above
411	O bless the Lord my soul
416	For the beauty of the earth
422	Not far beyond the sea
424	For the fruit of all creation
429	I'll praise my maker while I've breath
433	We gather together to ask the Lord's blessing
437, 438	Tell out my soul
463, 464	He is the Way
482	Lord of all hopefulness
488	Be thou my vision
490	I want to walk as a child of the Light
508	Breathe on me breath of God
534	God is working his purpose out
546	Awake my soul stretch every nerve
554	'Tis the gift to be simple
586	Jesus thou divine companion
593	Lord, make us servants of your peace
610	Lord whose love through humble service
611	Christ the worker
635	If thou but trust in God to guide thee
654	Day by day
659, 660	O Master, let me walk with thee
663	The Lord my God my shepherd is
664	My shepherd will supply my need
665	All my hope on God is founded
678, 679	Surely it is God who saves me
680	O God our help in ages past

From *Lift Every Voice and Sing II*

From *Wonder, Love, and Praise*

775	Give thanks for life (celebration of life, remembering the departed)
787	Siyahamba
790	Put peace into each others' hands
791	Peace before us
797	It's me, O Lord
800	Precious Lord, take my hand
805	I want Jesus to walk with me
808	Thuma mina
810	Eagles' Wings
811	Be not afraid
812	Here I am, Lord
819	Guide my feet, Lord

From *Voices Found*

60	Come and seek the ways of Wisdom
71, 72	Mothering God
81	Jesus, name above all names (for new name)
97	In deepest night (remembering a departed soul)
109	People of God (general)
113	Queremos cantar (general—image of each one having a calling)
121	Come, sing the joy of Miriam (general—image of journey)
127	Take my yoke upon you (good for retirement)
136	Mothers call upon the Maker (celebrating women's relationships)
138	I hope my mother will be there (remembering a departed soul)
139	Chun-guang ming-mei (Brilliant spring) (stages of life)
142	Bless now, O God, the journey (alternative tune in *Bring the Feast*)
145	Lo, the winter's past
149	I have borrowed him (rite of passage for young people and their parents)

From *With One Voice* (Evangelical Lutheran Church in America Supplement)

| 718 | Here in this place (Gather us in) |

The following are especially suitable for the rite of passage celebrating an engagement.

748	Bind us together
751	As man and woman we were made
749	When love is found
770	I was there to hear your borning cry
781	My life flows on in endless song

From *The Faith We Sing* (United Methodist Supplement)

2001	We sing to you, O God
2008	Let all things now living
2046	Womb of life
2051	I was there to hear your borning cry
2114	At the font we start our journey (*especially good during Easter season*)
2163	He who began a good work in you

From *The Presbyterian Hymnal*

192	God our Help and Constant Refuge (Psalm 46)
212	Within your shelter, loving God (Psalm 91)
238	Unless the Lord the house shall build (Psalm 127)
253	I'll praise my maker (Psalm 146)
294	Wherever I may wander
302	Lord of the Dance
335	Though I may speak (betrothal)
369	I'm gonna live so God can use me
384	O love that will not let me go (elders—celebration of life)
529	Lord of the living (remembering the departed)

From *The New Century Hymnal* (United Church of Christ)

362	When love is found (tune: *Waly waly*) (betrothal)
369	Keep your lamps trimmed and burning
370	What gift can we bring?
417	This is a day of new beginnings
429	God bless our homes
432	'Tis winter now (elders)
468	The care the eagle gives her young
564	We are not our own
583	Like a mother who has borne us

From *Gather Comprehensive*

649	You are mine
589	May the Lord, mighty God